Caves

Story by Veda Boyd Jones
Photography by Ryan Durney

Caves are holes in the ground.
Some caves are big.
Some caves are little.

Caves are dark.
There is no light in caves.

Bats live in caves. They fly out at night and eat insects.

Bears sleep in caves in winter. They come out in the spring.

Blind fish live in streams in caves. Their insides show through their skin.

People go in caves for fun, but they follow a rule.

Take nothing but pictures, leave nothing but footprints.

ESSENTIAL MARTIAL ARTS

Written by Simon Mugford
Designed by Barry Green and the Top That! team

TOP THAT! Kids™

Copyright © 2004 Top That! Publishing plc,
Top That! Publishing, 27023 McBean Parkway, #408 Valencia, CA 91355
Top That! is a Registered Trademark of Top That! Publishing plc
All rights reserved
www.topthatpublishing.com

Contents

Introduction	3
Martial Arts Philosophy	4
Religion	6
Styles, Etiquette, and Equipment	8
Weapon Arts	10
Empty-hand Arts	12
Chinese Martial Arts	14
Kung Fu	16
Chinese Kickboxing	18
Jeet Kune Do (JKD)	20
T'ai Chi	22
Japanese Martial Arts	24
Kendo	26
Ninjutsu	28
Judo	30
Aikido	32
Filipino Martial Arts (FMA)	34
Korean Martial Arts (KMA)	36
Tae Kwon Do	38
Tang Soo Do	40
Unusual Martial Arts	42
Celebrity Martial Artists	44
Glossary	46
Find Out More	48

Introduction

The word "martial" means "war-like," and the first martial artists developed their skills for use in battle.

Arts and Aims
Becoming a good martial artist takes years of practice, mental training and self-discipline—it is not simply about being able to defeat an opponent.

Asian Origins
The many forms of martial arts originated hundreds of years ago in Asia. China, Japan, Korea, and Thailand produced most of the best-known styles.

The ancient art of t'ai chi is a gentle, yet powerful, martial art.

World Sports
Martial arts are now extremely popular all over the world. Most disciplines have world championship competitions, while tae kwon do and judo are both represented at the Olympic Games.

Screen Stars
Since the 1970s, martial arts movies have helped to increase the popularity of certain styles. Kung fu expert Bruce Lee is probably the best-known of the martial arts movie stars.

Martial Arts Philosophy

Although many martial arts may appear to be aggressive, in reality their practice is based upon a thoughtful and philosophical approach.

Anti-Anger
Self-discipline, courtesy, and respect for others are central to all martial arts. The belief is that through training and study, the martial artist learns to control his or her aggression and becomes a more peaceful person. Martial arts are much more than hobbies; they are a way of life to followers.

Weapons and Moods
Even the styles that use weapons are concerned with bringing the body and mind into harmony. Although they may appear aggressive at first, this is misleading, because martial arts are as much about predicting and avoiding conflict as they are about dealing with it when it happens.

Inner Peace
Practicing meditation is important to the martial artist. It helps to bring inner peace and control aggression.

Confucianism
The teachings of Confucius—a 6th-century BC teacher and philosopher—influence the practice of many Chinese martial arts. Its main teaching is, "Never do to others what you would not like them to do to you."

Shorinji Kempo
Shorinji kempo is a martial art that has its origins in India over 5,000 years ago. It is said that the Buddha was so impressed by the art as a way of unifying the mind and body that he incorporated it into his teachings. Today there are many forms of kempo.

The lotus position is used in meditation.

Martial Arts Philosophy

Shinto
Many Japanese martial arts are based around the philosophies of the Shinto religion. Shinto is based on the worship of the gods of nature.

Zen Philosophy
Zen is a type of Japanese Buddhism. Its followers spend long periods of time in deep meditation—this helps to focus the mind away from the distractions of everyday life.

Zen Archery
Kyudo is a Japanese martial art that is a form of archery. It is practiced to increase mental discipline rather than as a sport. The way that the arrow is loaded and released is more important than accuracy.

Kyudo, a martial art which is also a form of archery.

Religion

Religion has a key role in the practice, study, and teaching of martial arts. Buddhism, which teaches self-discipline and mental awareness, is especially significant.

The Shaolin Temple.

Spiritual Art
Holy men traveled from India to China, taking the teachings of Buddhism with them. They learned martial arts as a way to defend themselves. To the true martial artist, the spiritual side of the arts is as important as the physical.

Traveling Monks
The Shaolin monks were famous martial artists. They traveled widely throughout Asia, introducing the arts to different countries. Their work continues today, as the monks put on martial arts displays around the world.

Shaolin Temple
The Shaolin Temple in China is one of the most important places in the world for martial arts. It is thought to be over 1,600 years old. Regarded as the ancient center for Chinese kung fu, the buildings spread out over 10,000 acres.

A Shaolin monk in action, breaking a concrete block with his head. ON NO ACCOUNT SHOULD YOU TRY THIS—IT IS PERFORMED BY TRAINED PROFESSIONALS ONLY AND IS EXTREMELY DANGEROUS.

Religion

Taoism
Chinese martial arts are closely linked to the Taoist religion. The yin/yang symbol of Taoism represents how strength is balanced with compassion and gentleness. Unlike other religions, Taoism does not consider good behavior as important as acting in harmony with nature. It is believed that by acting in harmony with nature good behavior will follow.

A student practicing t'ai chi.

Styles, Etiquette, and Equipment

There are many hundreds of styles of martial arts.

Hard and Soft
They can be broadly divided into "hard" styles—where punches, kicks, and strikes are practiced—and "soft" styles, which focus on the control of power. Many martial arts combine the two. Broadly, they can also be separated by country, as some martial arts are particularly associated with China, some with Japan, some with the Philippines, and others with Korea.

Bowing
Respect for your teacher and opponent is an important part of martial arts. In judo, students must kneel to bow to their teacher before a lesson. Opponents must make a standing bow to one another at the beginning and end of a contest. Bowing is really the equivalent to the ritual of shaking hands that takes place in other sports, such as football and tennis.

Clothing
Each martial art has a special kind of clothing. In judo and aikido, the suit is called a "judogi"—in karate it is called a "gi." It is made of heavy cotton fabric, which can withstand a lot of tugging.

The karate uniform worn when training.

8

Styles, Etiquette, and Equipment

Belt
The belt serves two purposes. It holds the jacket in place, and the color of the belt indicates the level of skill that the artist has reached. In judo, for example, artists progress from white to black belt. The belt is worn with pride.

Weapons
Many arts involve the use of weapons. Kendo, for instance uses a wooden sword called a "shinai." Most beginners will practice the art without weapons.

The bow (zarei) is done from the seiza (kneeling) position.

Weapon Arts

Weapons have a number of different roles in martial arts. Some styles, such as kendo, are based entirely around the use of a weapon.

Weapon Skills

Martial arts such as kung fu use weapon skills as part of the practice of self-defense. The student is taught to regard the weapon with respect. The study of traditional weapons helps the student to understand the dynamics of their body and how to generate power. The skills developed help to improve performance in the martial arts that don't use weapons.

Basics

In any of the weapon arts, students will learn basic techniques before they begin to handle weapons. This is as much for their own protection, as for their opponent's.

Kendo

Kendo is one of the most widely practiced of the weapons arts. It has its origins in the sword-fighting schools of the Japanese samurai. Kendo weapons include tanto, shoto, daito, and suburito sticks.

Jedi

Fans of the Star Wars movies will be familiar with some of the moves of kendo and other Japanese sword-fighting arts. They provided the inspiration for the famous light saber battle scenes.

The Japanese art of kendo.

Weapon Arts

Nunchakus, swords, and kamas are just some of the weapons used in martial arts.

Iaido
Iaido is "the art of drawing and attacking with the sword." It is mostly practiced alone —iaido is a test of imagination and concentration.

Moving Meditation
Weapon arts such as kendo and kyudo (Japanese archery) teach awareness and control of the body. The use of a weapon demands increased concentration and most martial arts focus on this side, rather than any aggressive use.

Stick Skills
The Filipino martial arts of escrima, arnis, and kali teach skills using simple rattan sticks. This has its origins in a period during which the people of the Philippines were banned from owning, or using, weapons.

Weapon arts teach awareness and control of the body.

Empty-hand Arts

The so-called "empty-hand" arts are mainly based on fighting with bare hands and feet.

Karate was little-known in the west until the early part of the twentieth century.

King Karate
Karate, one of the most widely practiced of all the martial arts, is the "king" of the empty-hand styles. The very name karate means "empty-hand." Empty-hand styles are taught as sport and as self-defense.

Karate
Karate began on the Japanese island of Okinawa during the 15th century. At the time, carrying weapons on the island was forbidden, so the people developed alternative ways of protecting themselves.

Four Styles
There are four styles of karate—"shotokan," "wado ryu," "shito ryu," and "goju ryu." There are some differences between the styles, but they share the basic principles of high-energy punches, kicks, and strikes.

Jujitsu uses throws, locks and holds.

Empty-hand Arts

This karate block is a "jodan uke" (upper block).

Karate Competition
Competitive karate is very fast. A bout will last two or three minutes, and points are scored according to technique and striking targets.

Jujitsu
Jujitsu is an ancient Japanese martial art, which uses a series of throws, locks, and holds. Its name means "gentle fighting art."

Past and Present
Jujitsu shares some of its roots with the very well-known sport of sumo wrestling, and forms the basis of modern judo. It is practiced mainly as a self-defense art.

Chinese Martial Arts

Many of the great martial arts originated in China. Indeed, the Shaolin monks, considered by many to be the masters of martial arts, were based in northern China.

enlightenment. He arrived at a monastery, where he taught the monks martial arts exercises in an attempt to increase their physical health.

Influence
The ancient culture, religion, and philosophy of this unique country has had an important influence on the world of martial arts.

Origins
According to legend, martial arts were introduced to China by a Buddhist traveling from India in search of

Wai-chia
The term wai-chia refers to the external "hard" styles of Chinese martial arts. These include some forms of kung fu, jeet kune do, and Chinese kickboxing. They are typically fast and aggressive-looking, though still philosophical in outlook.

T'ai chi is an internal martial art.

Kickboxing is now practiced throughout the western world.

Chinese Martial Arts

Nei-chia
Nei-chia are the internal "soft" styles. These include t'ai chi, pa kua chang, and fusing-i chuan. These are practiced for physical and mental exercise rather than as competitive sports or self-defense.

T'ai chi means practicing its principles, not only physically, but also in body and mind.

Kung Fu

Kung fu is one of the most widely practiced Chinese martial arts. There are several hundred forms of kung fu, but they share many basic principles.

Combination
It combines both soft and hard styles, mostly in the form of punches, kicks, strikes, and blocks. Kung fu means "done well."

Wing Chun
Wing chun is one of the best-known styles of kung fu. It was developed as a soft style by a woman called Yim Wing Chun. Wing Chun literally means "eternal springtime." Wing chun kung fu focuses on the center of the body to conserve energy.

The Chinese refer to kung fu as their "national martial art."

Close Range
Kung fu is practiced at very close range. This means that the attacks and the responses are very fast and it takes a lot of practice to work at high speed.

Punches
Wing chun kung fu punches are very effective. They use a throwing action that develops a lot of power, even over a small distance.

Kung Fu

Traditional kung fu is a way of attaining true development.

Animal Styles
Some moves are based on the actions of animals and birds. For instance, the crane uses a pecking action with the thumb and fingers while the snake springs towards the opponent with a fast strike.

Kung Fu Monks
The Shaolin monks developed many different styles of kung fu. The styles developed as they were taught to villagers throughout China.

A Shaolin monk performing kung fu.

Kicks
All the kicks in wing chun kung fu are aimed at areas below the waist. This helps the kung fu artist to maintain balance.

Blocks
A kung fu block not only deflects an opponent's attack, but it prevents them from guarding against a response. This is called "closing off."

17

Chinese Kickboxing

Various forms of kickboxing have been practiced in China for thousands of years.

Styles
As the styles have developed and grown in popularity, they have introduced elements from other martial arts, including kung fu, tae kwon do, wrestling, and western boxing. Kickboxing is practiced as a competitive sport —the two most popular forms are wu shu kwan and san shou.

Military Origin
The modern style of san shou was developed in the 1920s by the Chinese military. They wanted to create a practical form of defense that combined traditional martial arts philosophy with modern sports science and fitness.

Platform
Competitive san shou bouts take place on a platform—similar to a boxing ring without ropes. Competitors can score points by throwing their opponent from the platform!

Protection
The powerful kicks and punches used in kickboxing mean that protective gear must be worn. Padded headgear, gloves, and shoes protect the kickboxer from their attacker.

Kickboxers can generate great power.

Chinese Kickboxing

Sparring
Beginners will start with basic sparring. This involves learning how to throw and block simple kicks and punches.

Roundhouse
The high, spinning kick common to most forms of kickboxing is known as a roundhouse kick.

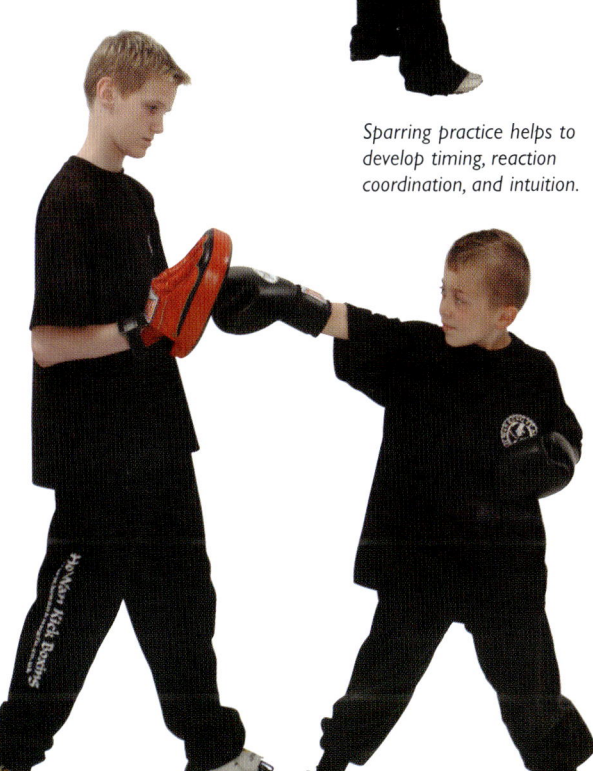

Sparring practice helps to develop timing, reaction coordination, and intuition.

Takedowns
A kickboxer performing a roundhouse kick is in a vulnerable position. If alert, the opponent can sweep their leg away, causing a takedown.

Body Locks
Wrestling-style body locks are taught in many types of Chinese kickboxing. However, they are left out of competitive bouts so that the action is not interrupted.

Competitors use 8 oz gloves for 145 pounds and under, and 10 oz gloves for 155 pounds and up.

Jeet Kune Do (JKD)

The martial art of jeet kune do was developed by Bruce Lee—probably the world's most famous martial artist.

Bruce Lee
Bruce Lee had trained in kung fu and studied many other martial arts and combat fighting sports. He found the rules and discipline of these styles restrictive, so he developed jeet kune do—"the way of the intercepting fist."

Street Style
Lee found that the rules of martial arts did not take into account the realities of street fighting, making them less effective as a means of self-defense. His aim was to develop a style that would prove effective in combat against fighters who were not following any rules.

No Rules?
The philosophy behind jeet kune do is that the student must train hard, learn what they can, then use only the things that suit them best. Lee believed that you should use your opponent's technique to create your own, saying "Your action should be as fast as a shadow adapting to a moving object."

One Move
Jeet kune do emphasizes fluidity and efficiency of movement. For instance, rather than blocking and punching in two moves, the whole action is done in one move.

Attack
Unlike other martial arts, the approach of jeet kune do is that attack is the best form of defense.

Bruce Lee founded the discipline of jeet kune do.

Jeet Kune Do (JKD)

Fighting Fit
Physical fitness is essential in jeet kune do, as the artist must react quickly. Both physical and mental speed are vital, as the artist must process the action in their head faster than their opponent.

Inside and Out
The practice of jeet kune do combines the concepts of the internal "soft" styles such as t'ai chi, with those of the external "hard" styles, such as kung fu.

JKD Today
Jeet kune do continues to be practiced in the way that Lee left it, but some practitioners have developed the style. Some military organizations and police forces train recruits in jeet kune do.

Jeet kune do is a self-defense-oriented martial art, using weapons (stick and knife).

T'ai Chi

T'ai chi is a popular form of the Chinese internal arts. It is based on the relationship between two opposing forces in nature, commonly described as yin and yang.

Taoist monks were first to practice the art of t'ai chi.

Calmness
T'ai chi combines relaxation and exercise in a series of continuous, flowing body movements. The art helps to cultivate a feeling of calmness.

Snake vs Crane
T'ai chi can be traced to a 12th-century Taoist monk called Chang San Fung. He created the art after seeing a fight between a snake and a crane.

Use the Force
T'ai chi is based on the principle of the soft overpowering the hard. In terms of combat, a t'ai chi artist will use their attacker's energy against them. Force is never met with force.

Inner Peace
The exercises associated with t'ai chi are also intended to promote a sense of well-being within the practitioner. By opening up to the ideas of t'ai chi, it is believed that you will become a better person.

T'ai chi is an exercise for relaxation, health, and self-defense.

T'ai Chi

Healing Art
T'ai chi is commonly practiced to help treat medical conditions. It is thought it can help increase blood circulation and develop flexibility. The slow, graceful nature of t'ai chi makes it popular with the elderly.

Starting Out
Learning t'ai chi begins with basic methods of aligning the body and maintaining balance. Slow, precise movement is the basis of the art, although some styles also include explosively fast moves.

Lower Strength
T'ai chi focuses on the legs and hips as a source of strength. This helps keep the body in a state of relaxation.

Public Arts
In China, t'ai chi is often practiced by large groups of people in squares and other public places, usually early in the morning.

The postures of t'ai chi balance yin and yang in the body.

Japanese Martial Arts

The Japanese martial arts date back more than 600 years. These arts, which are founded on the traditions of the ruling warrior classes, are known as "koryu bujutso."

Tradition
Respect for others has always been an essential part of the martial arts. Modern Japanese styles have continued that tradition.

Ryu
Japanese martial arts are taught at schools called "ryu." Most of these were created by noble samurai.

A Japanese samurai warrior.

Japanese Martial Arts

Training Hall
Japanese martial arts are taught and practiced in a special training hall called a "dojo." The dojo may differ according to the style being practiced. Where a lot of throwing takes place, as in judo, the dojo will have a padded floor.

Order and Respect
When entering and leaving the dojo, students must bow to the instructor. This is a sign of respect.

Students execute a standing bow (ritsu-rei) when entering and leaving the dojo, and at the start and end of a contest or practice.

Samurai
In ancient Japan, the samurai were a noble and respected class of warriors. For them, to die in battle would guarantee life in the next world. The samurai traditions are important in Japanese martial arts.

25

Kendo

Kendo—"the way of the sword"—is a Japanese weapon art, based upon the two-handed sword-fighting skills of the samurai.

History
Between the 14th and 16th centuries, sword skills were taught throughout Japan. The modern form of kendo was born in the 19th century and, by the 1950s, kendo had become part of the school curriculum.

Philosophy
Kendo emphasizes mental and physical strength and builds character, self-discipline, and respect—it is not practiced for self-defense.

Students of kendo.

Swords
Naturally, the use of real swords is very dangerous, so kendo uses a bamboo sword called a "shinai." Kendo artists also wear a range of protective clothing, collectively known as "bogu."

Headguard
The headguard used in kendo is called a "men." A scarf called a "tenegui" is worn inside the men. This cushions blows and soaks up sweat.

Kendo

Breastplate
The body protector is made up of a very soft, flexible "mune," and a plastic or bamboo breastplate called a "do."

Gloves
The gloves offer protection almost to the elbow. They are called "kote."

Shirts and Skirts
A special jacket called a "kendo-gi" is worn beneath the body armor. Loose-fitting skirts called "hakama" allow freedom of movement. The hips are protected by "tare."

Waza
The attack and defense movements in kendo are known as "waza." To be successful, artists must focus on their stance and footwork, and the technique of their cuts and thrusts.

Scoring Cuts
Points are awarded in competition for hitting certain targets with the right technique. The targets are the men, do, and kote.

Sword Technique
The correct technique involves using the left hand to power the sword and the right to control its direction.

Headguard ("men")

Scarf ("tenegui")

Breastplate ("do")

Gloves ("kote")

Skirt ("hakama")

swords

Ninjutsu

The Japanese martial art of ninjutsu has a somewhat mysterious and mystical nature.

Art of Stealth

Ninjutsu means "the art of stealth," and its early practitioners—ninjas—were experts in camouflage and secret undercover work. They were hired to carry out espionage (spying), and even contract killings. Such was the legendary status of the ninjas, it was widely believed that they were able to make themselves invisible.

Becoming Invisible

There are several tricks to moving without being seen, but one of the most important is to breathe in time with the movement of your body. Holding breath can cause muscle tension and may mean a noisy sharp intake of breath if you are startled.

A Japanese ninja.

Ninjutsu

Feuds and Families
Ninjutsu can be traced back to around 800 years ago when the samurai were the ruling class in Japan. Ninjas often formed families, or clans, who did not want to serve the samurai.

Disguise
The ninjas were masters of disguise and were able to blend into a community, adapting to almost any situation.

Weapons
Ninjutsu features an astonishing range of weapons and equipment—more than any other martial art. These range from "to ki"—climbing equipment—to the "hito washi," a type of board which, according to legend, enabled the ninja to hover above the ground.

The art of ninjutsu uses lethal weapons.

Judo

Judo is a very popular Japanese martial art based upon jujitsu. It was founded in 1882 by Dr. Jigro Kano, a university professor.

Origins
Dr. Kano took the less dangerous techniques of jujitsu and other styles, and refined them to form the modern style of judo. It is a safe but effective martial art, known for its impressive styles of throwing, grappling, and striking.

Gentle Art
Judo means "gentle way" and, as such, is a good martial art for beginners and children. However, judo competitions can still be quite vigorous.

Falling
The first thing that a judo student is taught is how to fall properly. The body needs to be relaxed and the arms should take most of the shock of hitting the ground. This is known as breakfalling.

Throwing
The aim of judo is to trip or throw your opponent to the ground and, if necessary, hold them in that position. There are three basic throws, known collectively as "nage."

Judo students must learn how to fall properly.

Judo

Striking
Striking moves, similar to those used in jujitsu, are still learned by some advanced judo artists. They are not permitted in competitive judo.

Grappling
Grappling, or groundwork, is known as "katame." Once your opponent is on the ground, the aim is to hold them in that position for 30 seconds. The basic technique involves holding your arm around your opponent's neck, and pressing your body weight against them.

Competitions
Points are awarded in judo competitions according to the quality of the throws and the groundwork. Tournaments, known as "shiai," range from small events to the Olympic Games. Typically, competitors fight someone who has the same belt as them and is of a similar weight.

Belts
There are seven colored belts awarded according to skill level. The order of colors is white, yellow, orange, green, blue, brown, and black. It takes years of practice to reach black belt.

Students must hold their opponent down for 30 seconds.

Aikido

Aikido is a graceful Japanese martial art known as "the way of harmony." Its basic philosophy is that force is never met with force.

Avoiding Action
Instead of using force, avoiding action is taken and the attacker's own force is used against them. For this reason, it is an excellent form of self-defense and is taught by many police forces around the world.

Origins
Aikido was founded by Morehei Ueshiba in the early 20th century. He was an expert in jujitsu, but wanted to create a means of defense that required little effort. Morehei Ueshiba is often called "O Sensei," meaning "Great Teacher."

Inner Energy
Learning aikido involves understanding the nature of an inner force known as "ki." Control of this force can be used against your opponent.

Techniques
Although aikido is based on avoiding action, it does involve throws and locks taken from jujitsu and other throws taken from kenjutsu.

A student and master practice aikido.

Aikido

Kata
Non-competitive aikido is known as "kata." In it the "nage" (defender) and the "uke" (attacker) display a number of moves of their choice in a time limit.

Competitive Aikido
There are three forms of competitive aikido. "Tanto randori" is fought over two rounds, with the uke armed with a rubber knife. "Randori kyoghi" is unarmed, while "ninindori" features three contestants.

Randori kyoghi is an unarmed form of aikido.

Filipino Martial Arts (FMA)

The islands of the Philippines are home to a distinctive style of martial arts.

Self-defense
There are several different types of Filipino martial arts—escrima, arnis, and kali are the best-known. These are self-defense arts that use both empty-hand styles and weapon techniques. Dumog, sikaran, and panantukan do not use any weapons. Filipino martial arts date from about the 9th century AD.

Simple Arts
Filipino martial arts were designed to be simple to learn. They were developed when the villages were under threat from invaders, and the people needed to learn quickly how to defend themselves.

Keep it Simple
The philosophy of simplicity remains today. Filipino martial arts are similar to Bruce Lee's jeet kune do, in that students are encouraged to work on the techniques that suit them best.

The use of one stick is called "baston."

Weapons or Not
Many of the techniques that involve weapons are the same, or very similar to those that do not. This means that practitioners can adapt to different self-defense situations without needing to know lots of different techniques.

Triangles
The triangle is an important symbol in the Filipino martial arts. It represents strength and many of the moves are based around a triangular pattern.

Live Hand
The "live hand" is an important concept in Filipino martial arts. It refers to the hand that does not contain the main weapon. It is used for checking, blocking, striking, and to assist with disarming and locks.

Filipino Martial Arts (FMA)

Sticks
The use of sticks is central to most of the Filipino martial art styles. "Baston" involves the use of one stick. Two sticks used in a crisscross style is called "sinawali."

Uniforms
Unlike martial arts such as judo, there is no requirement to wear a uniform. Artists may wear T-shirts if they wish. Shoes are always worn, to protect the feet and recreate conditions of day-to-day life.

Belts
It is only recently, as FMA have become more popular, that a ranking system based on belts has been introduced.

Filipino martial arts do not require uniform to be worn.

Filipino martial artists train with both weapons and empty hands.

35

Korean Martial Arts (KMA)

Various forms of martial arts have been practiced in the part of Asia now divided into North and South Korea for thousands of years.

Origins
The Japanese troops that occupied the area during the early 20th century introduced karate, judo, and kendo. Many new styles began to develop, among them hapkido, kuk sool won, hwa rang do, and tae kwon do.

Hapkido
Hapkido combines joint locks, pressure points, throws, kicks, and strikes for practical self-defense. It emphasizes circular motion and control of the opponent in a similar way to aikido.

The founder of hapkido was Yong Shul Choi, a Korean. It is likely that he was taken to work in Japan when he was a child.

Hwa Rang Do
Hwa rang do is a relatively modern art, developed in the 1960s. It involves unarmed combat, weapon skills, internal training, and healing techniques.

Kuk Sool Won
This style brings together parts of many traditional Korean styles. It focuses on mental and physical energy, along with meditation, acupuncture, and breathing exercises. Kuk sool won involves over 3,600 different techniques.

A heel kick in tae kwon do.

Korean Martial Arts (KMA)

Training Hall
The training hall or school where Korean martial arts are taught is called the "dojang," which translates as "school where the way is taught."

Etiquette
Etiquette plays an important role in Korean martial arts. When entering the dojang, the student should bow to the teacher. When the class is due to begin, the teacher will clap his hands and once again the students should bow. Students are expected to be disciplined and respectful throughout the class.

Belts
As with other martial arts, there is a belt ranking system. In tae kwon do the order is white, yellow, green, blue, red, and black.

Black is the highest-ranking belt in tae kwon do.

Korean martial arts balance physical power with mental power.

Tae Kwon Do

Tae kwon do means "the way of the foot and the fist." It is similar in many ways to karate and is famous for its range and quality of kicks.

Olympic Sport
Tae kwon do was officially sponsored by the Korean government during the 1950s, and this led to the creation of a formal teaching and grading system. One of the most popular martial arts in the world, in the year 2000 it became an Olympic sport.

General Choi
General Choi Hong Hi, an early pioneer of tae kwon do, is sometimes credited with naming the art. He formed the International Tae Kwon Do Federation (ITF) in 1966 to promote the art around the world.

Tae kwon do is famous for its kicks.

Sparring
Sparring involves two fighters practicing their techniques to develop timing, focus, and speed. In competitive sparring, points are scored when certain targets are struck with the correct technique.

Etiquette
As with all martial arts, etiquette is important. The suit (dobok) should be clean, no jewelry should be worn, proper bows should be made on entering and exiting the dojang, and unless it is absolutely necessary, there should be no talking.

Patterns
A series of set techniques performed against an imaginary opponent is known as a "pattern." One of the first patterns learned is "chon ji tul" —the "heaven and earth pattern."

Tae Kwon Do

Destruction
Practicing breaking objects, such as a piece of wood, is known as "destruction." This helps focus the mind and develop the effectiveness of a technique.

ITF Tae Kwon Do
In ITF tae kwon do competitions, the participants carry out low-impact attacks wearing head, fist, and foot protection.

Olympic/WTF Tae Kwon Do
The form of tae kwon do performed at the Olympics is a much more physical style. Full power kicks and punches to the head and body are allowed, though punches to the face are not. Protective headgear is worn.

Right middle section snap kick.

Tang Soo Do

Tang soo do is a classic Korean martial art. It means "way of the Tang hand," after the styles developed under the Tang dynasty in China.

Combination
Tang soo do is a combination of hard and soft styles with some soft, flowing movements. It uses a lot of foot techniques and is famous for its range of spectacular kicks.

Protection
Early versions of tang soo do have been traced to nearly 2,000 years ago. Originally people learned tang soo do to protect themselves from the samurai.

Board Breaking
As in tae kwon do, the power of a technique is demonstrated by smashing plastic boards.

Non-competitive
Tang soo do is a martial art in the classical sense—it is not a sport as such. Its main purpose is to improve and focus the emotions and spirit of those who practice it.

Strength is demonstrated through the breaking of boards.

Tang soo do combines hard and soft styles.

Benefits
The physical benefits you can expect from taking part in tang soo do include improved posture, flexibility, and stamina. Tang soo do also aims to teach concentration, self-discipline, and self-respect.

Tang Soo Do

Tang soo do is known for its flying, jumping, and spinning kicks.

Five Principles
All students of tang soo do must follow five basic principles:

1. Loyalty to one's monarch and country
2. Obedience to parents and elders
3. Respect to instructors and seniors
4. Self-control
5. Never misuse one's art

Unusual Martial Arts

The world of martial arts has some mysterious and unusual traditions.

Out of Practice
Arts such as karate, judo, and tae kwon do are very widely practiced and quite familiar, but there are some little-known styles that are so strange or so dangerous that they are no longer practiced.

Monkey Kung Fu
Known variously as tai sing mun, ta sheng, or dai shing pop gar, monkey kung fu is considered to be one of the strangest of all the martial arts. It is full of rolling and twisting movements, which are intended to confuse the opponent. Then a powerful kicking attack is made.

Kung Fu Styles
Other unusual kung fu styles include mantis kung fu, based on the attacking and defending techniques of the bird, and northern Shaolin kung fu, a "long-fist" technique that stresses the importance of kicking, rather than hand techniques.

Head Butt
Pachigi is a somewhat bizarre martial art from Korea. The basic style involves opponents head-butting one another—not recommended!

Kobujutsu
Kobujutsu, like karate, began on the Japanese island of Okinawa. The style of kobujutsu uses weapons such as the walking stick and the rice grinding handle.

Capoeira is a mixture of cartwheels, handstand, flips, and spinning kicks.

Unusual Martial Arts

Bone Breaking
Lua is a fabled martial art from the Pacific island of Hawaii. Its practitioners were said to be able to break the bones of their opponents without the use of weapons.

Extinct
Lua used the manipulation of pressure points to dislocate and break bones—fortunately it is now extinct.

Dancing Art
Capoeira is a Brazilian martial art, which appears very much like a form of dance. It is performed to music and is essentially a form of entertainment.

Danger Dance
Despite appearances, capoeira is very dangerous, as rapid kicks are delivered to the head—one of the most important parts of the body.

Capoeira uses incredible movements.

Celebrity Martial Artists

Martial arts movies have single-handedly increased interest in the arts outside of Asia.

Most of the martial arts superstars were very accomplished artists before becoming movie stars, and some of them, such as Bruce Lee, developed their own styles and philosophies.

Bruce Lee
Bruce Lee was the original martial arts superstar. He is often said to be responsible for raising the profile of martial arts around the world. He died in 1973, the year his famous movie *Enter the Dragon* was released.

Underdog
Lee was short and skinny, but his awesome kung fu skills made him unbeatable. He always appeared to be the underdog—this probably helped to make his movies so successful.

Jackie Chan
Jackie Chan studied a number of martial arts, notably kung fu and hapkido, and made his name as a stuntman in Hong Kong-produced kung fu movies.

Hollywood Star
After appearing in the Bruce Lee movies *Fist of Fury* and *Enter the Dragon*, Chan moved to the USA, where he has since become a major Hollywood star. His movies are noted for their speed and comic touches.

Bruce Lee.

Jackie Chan.

Celebrity Martial Artists

Chuck Norris
Chuck Norris, who starred in numerous action movies throughout the 1970s, 1980s, and 1990s, started out as a karate and tang soo do champion. He made his breakthrough in Bruce Lee's *Return of the Dragon*.

Chuck Norris.

Jet Li
Jet Li trained extensively in Shaolin and wu shu kung fu. He is credited with rekindling the interest in martial arts during the 1980s. Li has starred in numerous

Jean-Claude Van Damme
Jean-Claude Van Damme has starred in a number of martial arts movies, including *No Retreat, No Surrender,* and *Kickboxer*. Van Damme had studied karate since the age of ten, becoming European middleweight champion before moving into movies.

Hollywood movies, including *Lethal Weapon 4* and *Romeo Must Die*.

The Karate Kid
Ralph Macchio starred as *The Karate Kid* in 1984, as a victim of bullying who learns karate. Not only does his new skill help him to take on the bullies, but also he learns that there is more to martial arts than fighting.

The Magnificent Seven
The classic holiday movie, *The Magnificent Seven*, was based on a Japanese movie, *The Seven Samurai*, about warriors defending a village from bandits.

Jet Li.

Glossary

Here you will find the styles and country of origin of all the martial arts styles mentioned in the book.

China

Dai shing pop gar	monkey kung fu—empty-hand, hard, external
Fusing-i chuan	soft, internal
Hsing i	soft, internal
Jeet kune do	empty-hand, soft/hard, external/internal
Kung fu	empty-hand, soft/hard, external/internal
Pa kua	empty-hand, soft, internal
San shou	type of Chinese kickboxing—hard, external
Shaolin	type of kung fu—empty-hand, hard, external
T'ai chi	empty-hand, soft, internal
Ta sheng	monkey kung fu—empty-hand, hard, external
Tai sing mun	monkey kung fu—empty-hand, hard, external
Wing chun	type of kung fu—empty-hand, hard, external
Wu shu kwan	type of Chinese kickboxing—hard, external

Judo is a Japanese art.

Glossary

Japan

Aikido	empty-hand, hard, external
Iaido	weapon art, soft, internal
Judo	empty-hand, soft, external
Jujitsu	empty-hand, soft, external
Karate	empty-hand, hard, external
Kobujutsu	weapon art, hard, external
Kendo	weapon art, hard, external
Kyudo	weapon art, soft, internal
Ninjutsu	weapon art/empty-hand, soft/hard, internal/external
Shorinji kempo	empty-hand, hard, external

Korea

Hapkido	empty-hand, hard, external
Hwa rang do	empty-hand, hard, external
Kuk sool won	empty-hand, hard, external
Pachigi	empty-hand, hard, external
Tae kwon do	empty-hand, hard, external
Tang soo do	empty-hand, hard, external

Philippines

Arnis	weapon art, hard, external
Escrima	weapon art, hard, external
Kali	weapon art, hard, external

Find Out More

If you think you've got what it takes to become the next Bruce Lee, then why not keep up-to-date on all the latest news?

Bookshops
Bookshops carry, or can order, specialist martial arts magazines and books. You could visit your local library to see what they have to offer.

Clubs
You can join local clubs, where you'll be able to learn martial arts under the supervision of a professional teacher.

Internet
Find out about martial arts on the internet. Ask an adult to help you search for websites.

Picture Credits
The publisher would like to thank the following contacts and organizations for their involvement, help, and co-operation in creating this project:

- the students of **Hollesley Judo Club** and **Ho Wan Kung Fu Academy**.

- **Combat**—Martial Arts Magazine. Editor—Paul S. Clifton, 135 Aldridge Road, Perry Barr Birmingham, England B42 2ET. Tel 0121 344 3737 www.martialartsinprint.com
Pics: Chinese kick boxing, Tang Soo Do Luha, Escrima, Kali, Ju Jitsu, Laido, Hapkido, Kuk Sool Won, Jeet Kune Do.

- **All Star Picture Library**: pics of Jet Li, Chuck Norris, Bruce Lee, Jackie Chan.

- **Getty Images**: pic of Taoist monk.

- **Action Plus**: Tai Chi (Neale Haynes) Shaolin Kungfu (Glyn Kirk), Taekwondo (Tony Henshaw), Kendo (Mile Hewitt), Kick Boxing (Neil Tingle), Aikido (J M Emportes/DPPI), Capoeira (Franck Faugere/DPPI).